SUMANA
THE FLORIST

©2015 All Rights Reserved

ISBN: 978-955-687-039-8

Computer Typesetting by

Mahamevnawa Buddhist Monastery, Toronto
Markham, Ontario, Canada L6C 1P2
Telephone: 905-927-7117
www.mahamevnawa.ca

Published by

Mahamegha Publishers
Waduwawa, Yatigaloluwa, Polgahawela, Sri Lanka.
Telephone: +94 37 2053300 | 77 3216685
www.mahameghapublishers.com
mahameghapublishers@gmail.com

SUMANA
THE FLORIST

*With the guidance and direction of
Most Venerable Kiribathgoda Gnānānanda Thera*

Artwork by Sumathipāla & Jothipāla

A Mahamegha Publication

Sumana the Florist

My dear sons and daughters, when it comes to performing meritorious deeds, some don't get the opportunity. Some have to put in a lot of effort and make huge sacrifices. To do that, a person must have great confidence in merit.

This story tells you about a person who sacrificed his life to perform merit.

He lived in the town of 'Rajagaha' and his name was 'Sumana'.

His job was supplying Jasmine flowers to King Bimbisara. Every day he took eight quarts of flowers to the palace. In return he received eight gold coins.

On this particular day Sumana the Florist was carrying the eight quarts of flowers in a basket placed on his head, to the palace. At the same moment the Supreme Buddha was walking along a street of Rajagaha. However, there was a difference on that particular day. A six coloured aura was emanating from the Buddha's body.

Sumana the Florist

Normally, the Buddha walks in such a way that nobody can detect any extraordinary feature. It's only on certain special days that the Buddha shows this miracle when walking. On such days, something special definitely happens and many people realize Dhamma.

On that special day, the Buddha's body emanated six colours - blue, yellow, red, white, orange and a blend of those five colours. As the Buddha walked by, people were inspired by this sight and expressed their happiness by saying "Sadu, Sadu, Sadu".

Sumana, the Florist saw this. Quickly, he placed his basket of flowers on the ground, knelt down, opened his eyes wide and looked at the Supreme Buddha in astonishment. His heart overflowed with faith and respect towards the Buddha. He felt goose bumps on his body and his body hair straightened out. The joy in his heart was so much that tears flowed from his eyes. "Oh, my Supreme Teacher is unmatched, not only in wisdom; my Supreme Teacher is unmatched in emanating the aura of colours from His body.

Sumana the Florist

The Pinnacle of the three worlds.. my Lord Buddha… is the most suitable to receive veneration and offerings of Gods and Brahmas. Oh! …. look …. look, how wonderfully the six colours are emanating!! If only I could offer something..!

But I only have these Jasmine flowers with me, and these flowers are for the king. If I don't take them, the king will definitely punish me. He will harass me. He will put me in jail. Oh! What should I do? What is the use of my life if I don't offer something now!

No ….No, none of that matters to me. If the king puts me in jail, let him do so. If he expels me from the country, let him expel me. If he beheads me, let him do so. None of that matters right now. I am going to offer these flowers to the Supreme Buddha..yes…and not only that, I will offer my life as well to the Buddha".

Sumana the Florist

Just then the Buddha walked towards Sumana the Florist. Sumana quickly took two quarts of flowers in both hands and threw them to the sky saying;

"Dear Lord, the Fortunate One, walking by, displaying miracles, luminescent, radiating the six hues of the Buddha rays, bringing solace to the three worlds, Teacher of Gods and humans, Teacher of mine, I offer these Jasmine flowers to the Lord Buddha. Let them be offered to You! I offer my life as well! Let it be offered to You, Lord Buddha! Let this be for the well being of all living beings...!"

The two quarts of Jasmine flowers he threw to the sky shouting thus, did not fall to the ground. Instead, they formed a canopy in the sky. Overwhelmed by that sight people around chanted very loudly; "Sadu, Sadu, Sadu".

Sumana the Florist was overjoyed and took another two quarts of Jasmine flowers in both hands. He threw them to the right side of the Buddha and they formed a beautiful curtain of Jasmine flowers on the right side. Then he took another two quarts in his hands and threw them to the left side of The Buddha. These too appeared as a beautiful curtain of flowers on the left side.

Sumana the Florist

There was another thing special about all this. When the Supreme Buddha walked by, these Jasmine flowers moved forward with Him. When The Buddha stopped, the Jasmine flowers stopped as well. The news of the miracle of Jasmine flowers spread all over the town of Rajagaha like a pleasant fragrance.

The news of the Jasmine flower miracle reached the King's palace too. The King also hurried to see this miracle. Everyone was amazed by this. The King did not know that those flowers were meant for him. That day the King did not receive any Jasmine flowers. Sumana the Florist went home joyfully. Then his wife asked him;

"What happened? Didn't you take the flowers today"?

"No .... today I offered those flowers to the Supreme Buddha. It doesn't matter what happens to me now. Even if I have to die.. it does not matter to me. My mind is serene today. I have collected my merit".

The Florist's wife got really scared and looked at him with wide eyes. She was so distressed and started crying and quarrelling with him.

Sumana the Florist

"Oh..what have you done? What a stupid person you are..! What are we going to tell the King? Oh...the king will be angry with us, we will be punished. Oh..! we are all ruined. There is nothing that I can do. I will inform the King about this".

Saying thus, the wife went to the palace crying, carrying her infant and holding the other child by the hand. She fell on her knees in front of the King and worshipped him. Then she said to the King;

"Oh Your Majesty, the great King, please have compassion on your servant. This man has come home empty handed, having offered the eight quarts of Jasmine flowers due to you, to the Buddha. This is not an intentional wrong doing. Now our whole family is going to be ruined by what this man has done. Your Royal Highness, have compassion on this foolish act".

Then King Bimbisara asked ;

"What.... what did you say? Did you say that the Great Teacher was offered the Jasmine flowers which were brought for me?

Sumana the Florist

Dear woman, I am the one who should have made that sacred offering to my peerless Leader. Sumana has done something that I should have done. Sumana the Florist has definitely done a great meritorious deed. Sadu! Sadu! I share the merit. Now, don't be a useless, foolish woman. At least now, share the merit that your husband has gained".

The King went to see the Lord Buddha and told Him about this incident. That special day, the canopy of Jasmine flowers moved up to the main gate of Veluwanarama. The King shared the great merit which was brought about by the actions of Sumana the Florist.

"Dear Lord, the Fortunate One, this person has definitely sacrificed his life to perform this merit. Therefore, as a mark of respect, I will offer him a life full of comfort and riches worth eighty-four thousand gold coins, a luxurious palace, a group of villages and I will also offer him the status of 'Regional Ruler'."

By and by, Sumana the Florist became Baron Sumana. Everyone was so happy about the great meritorious deed that Sumana the Florist performed.

Bhikku Ananda asked the Supreme Buddha ;

"My Lord, from today onwards, Sumana the Florist is a 'Baron'. Isn't it the consequence of the meritorious deed he performed?"

"Dear Ananda, this is only a miniature return yet. Because of the way he made his mind faithful towards me, his next birth will definitely be a special birth.

As a consequence of his meritorious deed, he will be born in heavenly abodes for a hundred thousand aeons. He will enjoy a luxurious life among gods and humans. In his last birth, he will be born as a Private Buddha by the name of 'Sumana'." The Buddha also stated,

"If something is done, it should be done without regret, and it should only be something that brings happy returns, which can be enjoyed with a happy mind". Saying thus, The Supreme Buddha chanted this stanza;

Thancha Kamman Kathan Sadhu
Yan Kathwa Nanuthappathi
Yassa Pathitho Sumano
Wipakan Patisewathi

Sumana the Florist

Thus meritorious deeds - bring comforts abundantly
He who does collect merits - enjoys comforts
Therefore, it's always best – to make a point in your life
To hasten in righteous acts – that gives much merits.

My dear children, this discourse on merits expounded by the supreme Buddha was very useful to many. Sumana the florist had no aspiration to become a Private Buddha. All he did was form a pleasant mind with great respect towards the supreme Buddha. It was the supreme Buddha who proclaimed the prophecy that such great human beings appear in the world from time to time. And that Sumana the florist will be one of them in the future.

Therefore, the supreme Buddha walked in the streets of Rajagaha that day, exhibiting a colourful aura, for the benefit of Sumana the florist. Upon listening to the Dhamma explained to Sumana, eighty four thousand people realized the Dhamma that day and became stream-entrant, Sothapanna, disciples of the supreme Buddha.

Accordingly, how wonderful it would be if we too can gain such comforts and happiness by learning this noble Dhamma and performing meritorious deeds!

Mahamegha English Publications

Sutta Translations
Stories of Sakka, Lord of Gods: Sakka Saṁyutta
Stories of Great Gods: Brahma Saṁyutta
Stories of Heavenly Mansions: Vimānavatthu
Stories of Ghosts: Petavatthu
The Voice of Enlightened Monks: Theragāthā

Dhamma Books
The Wise Shall Realize

Children's Picture Books
The Life of the Buddha for Children
Chaththa Manawaka
Sumana the Novice Monk
Stingy Kosiya of Town Sakkara
Kisagothami
Kali the She-Devil
Ayuwaddana Kumaraya
Sumana the Florist
Sirigutta and Garahadinna
The Banker Anāthapiṇḍika

To order, go to www.mahamevnawa.lk

www.ingramcontent.com/pod-product-compliance
Lightning Source LLC
Chambersburg PA
CBHW041235040426
42444CB00002B/172